I0476599

# MANAGEMENT

## Everything is always your fault!

## Disagree?

# DON'T BE A MANAGER

### Ozzie Sollien

For any questions or comments, you may contact the author at ozziesollien@gmail.com.

Copyright©2015 Ozzie Sollien
All rights reserved

ISBN-13: 978-1514249932
ISBN-10: 1514249936

# TABLE OF CONTENT

Cover picture:  Stock photo.

## INTRODUCTION

This book is dedicated to one of my management teams in the United States: Region Manager Peter Roughan of Dover, New Hampshire and Branch Manager James Dunn of Baltimore, Maryland. They made a series of statements about management which I call "The Roughan-Dunn Doctrine" (the Rowan-Dunn Doctrine). I regard the statements as my golden rules of management. They are all very simple. The first time I heard them I automatically disregarded them as either being incorrect, or impossible to live by. Over time, however, I came to learn that the statements were indeed very true, and my ultimate success was unconditionally dependent on accepting them as imperative cornerstones in building my own management strategy.

The most important of them all was the title: "It is always the manager's fault". I had to make that my mission statement. Only then could I seriously approach the task at hand – to learn how to manage, and how to be successful at management.

The skills of the ideal manager has been very well conceptualized by my good friend David McLenachan, retired Commercial Director for Initial Technical Services in the United Kingdom:

*The very best managers can inspire you and make you work better, or harder. They do that by connecting to you, leading by example and having ideas and innovations that you can see are valid attempts to move the business for-*

*ward. They work alongside you, are not lazy, are account-able themselves and not afraid to be so even in full view of their people. Above all else they are good communicators, demanding, but in a good, fair manner and they conduct themselves in a professional way.*

This is not a book written just to make it easier for you to manage. It is a book written to get ideas about how to look deep into yourself, to see which of your acquired experiences you can combine and the changes you can make within your mind to become a truly good and successful manager.

Salford, Manchester
United Kingdom
July 2015

Ozzie Sollien

## GOLDEN GUIDELINES OF MANAGEMENT

Throughout the book these golden guidelines are high-lighted with an "x" and written in bold, italic letters.

*Be good to the good guys and bad to the bad guys.*

*Do not fix what is not broken.*

*Do not manage things. Manage people to do things.*

*If it looks like a duck, behaves like a duck and sounds like a duck – it is a duck!*

*If I could do without you for that long, I could do without you altogether.*

*If you are not early, you are late.*

*If you always do what you always did, you always get what you always got.*

*Inspect what you expect.*

*Just go there. The important thing is that you show up. It shows that you care!*

*Perception is reality.*

*The inmates are running the asylum.*

*The more you do, the more you get done. The less you do, the less you get done.*

*The one who picks up the phone first, wins.*

*The one who talks first, loses.*

*The road to Hell is paved with good intentions.*

*There are too many chiefs and not enough Indians.*

*Today is the first day in the rest of your life.*

*We have really good people, so we only have to reiterate ten times.*

*You can teach people how to do the job, but you cannot teach them attitude.*

*You cannot change people – only manage their behavior.*

At last a <u>counter productive</u> technique, sometimes observed among managers:

*Do what I say, not what I do.*

## WHAT IS MANAGEMENT *NOT* –
## AND IF IT IS NOT THAT – WHAT *IS* IT?

Both managers and people not involved in management may find the answer surprising:

**Management is <u>not</u> a platform created for you to wield power over your team members.**

Management is a lot of different things, but it is **not** that. It **can be** used for that purpose, and historically it **has very much** been used for that purpose, and occasionally **you may have to** use it for that purpose –

but that is not what it <u>**is**</u>,

Corporate structures, often by default, used to endorse the paradigm of power in management as a tool to be held over employees. Managers tended to manage exclusively **up** – to be catering to their bosses, and to be slightly or decidedly condescending to their teams. Sadly, however, power as a tool in management is useful for one single purpose:

**To keep people down and in their place.**

Is that what you want to do? Do you not want your organization to –

Thrive?
Increase?

Expand?
Be successful?

How do you achieve that with people who feel **trapped under power?**

Management is **coaching and tutoring your team** with the goal of teaching them everything **you** know, so **they** in turn can apply it to a much larger group of customers than **you** can do **yourself**, because **you** are only <u>**one**</u> **person.** This is what I call

**managing up by managing down,**

which means:

By educating and managing **your** people to be successful and reach desired results, **you** will satisfy the demand of your upper management. Through the success of **your** team, **you** clearly show **your** capability for success.

In my 30 years in business - both in Europe and the United States - the single most common answer when new emp-loyees were asked what they wanted to achieve in the com-pany was:

"I want to get into management".

If this is the first thing on your mind when accepting a new position, you have not fully understood the concept of ma-nagement and what it requires. Management is not some-thing you "get into". You get into a car. You do not get in-to management. The response indicates an urge to get aw-ay from everyday business, isolate yourself from people you manage, get above the currents of daily duties and make as much money as possible, doing as little as possible.

The attitude of wanting to create a gap – or a distance – between managers and employees I found to be much more prevalent in "older" corporate cultures. That is **not** the way to manage. The only management taking place is to manage to get away from responsibility.

A good answer from someone anticipating a career in management would be:

**"I want to learn as much as possible. I want to interact with my co-workers as much as possible, so I get a good impression of how everything works. I want to interact with our customers as much as possible, to find out what they expect. Then – if or when I get promoted - I will have the ability to present myself to our customers both personally *and through my team, as they are the extension of me, when in contact with those customers*".**

This is **the only way** to become a good manager. You have to **know all the ins and outs** of what you are managing – your human resources, operational tools and customer scenarios. **Only then** can you make quick decisions, correct decisions and good decisions. And - you will **not** get away from everyday business - as a matter of fact, you will be far more involved in it than you ever were at a lower level in the hierarchy. You will be correcting and covering all the shortcomings and errors of the people you manage while they learn, to make it **your** organization, so it will work the way **you** want it to work. If not – and you might as well face it now - **you will not become a good mana-**

**ger.**

If you want to be a manager - a real manager and a succ-essful manager – forget about regular routines in your life, not involving work. Forget about coming home for dinner at the same time every day. Forget about regular holidays. And above all - forget about all the books telling you that you can actually be **so organized**, that you can put virtu-ally a weeks' worth of work into a 9 hour day. You cannot.

You will have to work long days to get everything done – you will have to put your nose to the grindstone and keep it there for 16 to18 hours a day. You will have to work during evenings and weekends. You can never turn your phone off.

Management is not something you **DO**.
Management is something you **ARE**.

It is a way of life, to the exclusion of everything else. If you cannot see that, you are not going to be a good man-ager. So make your choice now, because when you have, there is no going back - unless you want to drop out of real management.

You have just read the basics of the operational mechanics of management. After reading it, if you say to yourself: "I don't think I have to do all that" – stop reading. You will fail. If you say: "I think I can do that" – then we can get into what it really takes of you, as a human being, to be a good, successful manager.

## BE GOOD AT WHAT YOU DO

There is an old saying going like this:

**Whatever you do – be the best you can be.**

You cannot be respected as a manager unless you show that you are good in your field. You do **not** have to be the best, but you **have** to have a good understanding of what you are good at - and even more importantly – you **have to** know what you **do not** have a good grip on in your field. This is where you place effort on developing **yourself**.

Read up on everything you can find in **your** field. Avoid popular magazines with flashing titles about Super Managers who went from rags to riches in a month and everybody being in awe of them. They do not exist. The stories are purely created to sell magazines. **Do not** read them.

Read trade magazines, scientific periodicals, books written specifically about **your** field by people who have experience in **your** field. Couple that knowledge with what **you** see and learn **in** that field.

It is important to understand that neither of the two facets – theoretical knowledge or field experience - **alone** will make you a good manager. You can have vast theoretical knowledge, but if you have **no** field experience – you **cannot** apply it effectively, properly and correctly!

On the flip side: You can have many years of field experience, but without any theoretical knowledge - over time - you **will** make the mistake of drawing conclusions made on a few, selected incidences which will prove to be wrong and give you a misconception about how things work. If you place **those** observations at the foundation of your management strategy, you are **bound to** go wrong!

For the correct conclusions to be drawn and the proper decisions made, theoretical knowledge from samples of material collected from a vast array of incidences over an extended period of time **have to** be matched with knowledge gained by field experience.

Those sample collections can **only** be found in books and trade magazines. The field experience is **your** field experience.

**Combine** <u>those</u> **two facets, and mold them into YOUR own management strategy.**

Managers are often worried about hiring team members who have more knowledge than themselves. They fear competition.

**Never** fear competition. You **should** hire people with more knowledge about certain elements of your operation than yourself. They will become important members of the task force you are creating, helping **you** to reach the goals **you** cannot reach **alone**! This is **why** you hire good people. **Always** hire as good people as you can possibly find. **You** are the manager. **You** are the one to manage them – it is not a question of competition or fight for position. It is **your** team. **You** manage it.

Later these members may want to leave the team – to continue on a different path with the knowledge they have gained. **Let them**. Is that not what you would do? This is how careers are created – they develop from the dynamics of working in teams with different people who are good at different things, from whom you can learn. From there you carry on in different directions.

# RESPONSIBILITY

Let us talk about responsibility – the title of the book.

When something goes wrong with your team it is **always your fault**. Just accept it as a fact of life.

**You <u>automatically and immediately</u> take responsibility and instantly get on the task of putting it right.**

In creating a successful organization -

**time is your number one enemy**.

Expenses are running – fast. You have to create revenue - even faster. This is the reason why you have to **learn quickly and act decisively**.

**Do not waste time** -

by resisting the assumption of responsibility, trying to explain what happened and how it happened for the purpose of dispersing responsibility - **just start working on the solution.**

**NOW**.

If -

You cannot accept to be a chopping block.

You have a need to defend yourself.
You are self-righteous.
You have a need to organize things to set them right for yourself –

**do not** become a manager.  As a matter of fact:

**You will not be able to become one**.

<u>Here is why it is your fault:</u>

You did not teach your people what they needed to know.
You did not train them well enough.
You did not go out in the field to follow up, and see that they carried out what you taught them.
You did not make sure they carried out what you taught them, correctly.
You did not provide them with the tools and knowledge they needed, to do it correctly.

If you **did** do all those things, and it **still** went wrong –

**You hired the wrong people.**

You need to become a much better recruiter. Improve your interviewing skills. Recognize applicants at the table who will **not** be able to do the job satisfactorily

If you interviewed correctly, you dropped the ball after the interviewing process - and you can start on the list above, going in a circle.

**<u>It is always your fault</u>**.

# SUPPORT – INTERNAL CUSTOMER SERVICE

Two of the most important facets under the big umbrella of management are CUSTOMER SERVICE and SALES.

When hiring for an organization, you hire specific people for their customer service skills, and specific people for their sales skills. **YOU**, on the other hand, have to be **THE** best customer service representative **AND** the best sales representative of them all. You – **the manager** - have **two** separate groups of customers who will require both your excellent customer service skills and your superior sales skills. **You** have both internal and external customers.

The members of your team are your **internal customers.** The ones who are paying for your services are your **external customers**.

Let us start with the internal customers, your team.

First and foremost, **you** have to cater to the needs of your **internal** customers, the needs making **them** – and **you** – successful. You will only be successful through them – your success is going to need a team effort, and <u>**one,**</u> **meaning you alone**, is not a team. You have to manage the team well, both for them and for you, and you do that with **excellent internal customer service.**

<u>Why is your customer service to your team so important, and how do you exercise it?</u>

If you do not cater to your internal customers' needs – why would they cater to yours, and go the extra mile you want them to go, to achieve results and success? **Why**? Why would they not rather just wait impatiently for Friday, take their pay check and go home, and hate looking forward to Monday?

By catering to their professional and personal needs you create commitment. Commitment to their jobs. Commitment to the direction you want them to go. But first and foremost –

**commitment to YOU**.

If you have their commitment, and you lead – they will follow. Not only will they follow, they will charge ahead of you, if they see the goal **you** see.

Make internal customer service **personal**, just like the external. Praise your team members. Give them tokens of appreciation. Bring food if you go to their place of work in the field. Buy them a coffee. Make a point of remembering their birthdays. Give them a bottle of wine and a card. It costs **NOTHING**, and will pay for itself a thousand times over.

Show them that you care about them. They will be more productive. More focused. They pay more attention to important details. The details **YOU** have defined as important. They come to work even if they do not feel good, because they are committed. **TO YOU**. If you show them that you care about them, they will care about you, and help **you** improve.

**How** do you make them see the goal?

This is where your sales skills come into play:
You sell it to them. You sell them the idea of how great the accomplishment will feel, when they reach that goal.

It is not hard. Be you. Be open. Be inclusive. Show them that

**YOU are going there, no matter what**.

Smile. Praise – everything. Add caveats – prices, awards, appreciation. Ask for advice. People like to be asked for advice. You do not necessarily have to use it. Above all else – and again:

**Above all else – LISTEN**.

Listen. If somebody wants to tell you something, always listen. People like to have input. To voice their opinion. To contribute. My rule of thumb is:

In a conversation with my team I will have to listen to 80% of the issues I am already aware of - but among the **last 20%** are the real nuggets – the thoughts, ideas and experiences that **I can benefit from** -

**but I have to patiently listen to the 80%, to get the 20%!**

In a team of field representatives I found that after they started fresh in their job, he or she would spend a full year coming into my office, talking after work.

Why would I accept that? How could I stand it?

Because it was incredibly educational! **All** I had to do was to listen. I learned everything about my customers' premises, problems, habits, family, personal life and their preferences for how they wanted the service done. I learned this because my team developed a personal relationship with my customers, **by frequent contact**, which I did not have the opportunity to establish.

**Still, I got all the information I needed, as if _I_ had the relationship!**

This is true not only for the team members going out in the field, but also for your customer service representatives, being on the phone with your external customers. They often get frustrated. They want to talk about it. Listen. **Listen**. By listening to them venting their frustration, you will gather **incredible amounts of information**. Not only about your customers, but also about your CSRs, about how they think, how they talk and how they act,

**and from that you plan your management strategy**.

Managers will often say: I don't have time to do that - I cannot listen to all the petty talk coming from the CSRs and the field representatives. I have more important things to do.

No you don't. NO, you don't. No, **you do not**.

**This is how you learn**, from people who have direct contact with the customer 8-10 hours a day, every day. Would it not be good if **you** could spend time with **all** of your customers, **every day**, to know all their wants and needs, to be able to -

Sell more.
Do better service.
Be more productive.
Be more effective.
Grow faster.
Have more satisfied customers.

But **you** are only **one** person.
**How** can you do it?

**You do it by listening to the people who <u>ARE</u> at your customers every day.**

If you have a team of 10 field representatives, spending 10 hours a day with the customers, that equals 100 hours a day, 500-600 hours a week. Can you imagine the amount of information you can get out of those 500 - 600 hours, which **you**, as only **one person**, would have to spend **10 continuous weeks** to get?

You can **never** get all that information and take action on it **alone.** If you want to

Improve.
Learn more.
Manage better, and
do it QUICKLY –

**use the resources you have:**

**Your people.**

Put the information to good use by improving the already existing service and to sell and service more. You can go out and offer you external customers **exactly** what they want and how they want it, since you **already know** what it is. They will willingly pay, when they get exactly what they want.

You should not only **passively** receive information about all facets of your organization. You should **actively seek information** by orchestrating scenarios where you know your team will find this information **for** you. Tell them to ask certain questions and check on certain issues to find out the state of your operation. How was Mrs. Jones? Is Mr. Brown still having problems? Did Mrs. Smith get her basement fixed?

× *do not manage things. Manage people to do things.*

This is why you have to be a good customer service representative for your team – your **internal** customers. Why would they talk to you if you ignore them? Why would they give you all this information, help you learn all you need to learn and change everything you need to change if you **do not listen** to them – if you **just ignore them** and go home? **WHY**?

**You have to cater to your internal customers' needs and wants for your benefit. And for theirs.**

Communicate continuously to keep yourself current with all information you can possibly gather. Use all this information to manage the CSRs and the field representatives. Use it to make them as customer service oriented as possible, as effective as possible and to create even better service for your external customers.

**All the information about how to do that is right there, in front of you. The information is supplied to you by the active participants. Use it.**

The following technique is a major key to understand any situation you are trying to manage, involving several layers of the team, and external customers:

First listen to the field representatives. Then listen to the CSRs telling you the same story. Then listen to the customer. Now you will get a profound appreciation for the concept that

× *perception is reality*.

**What they are telling you are three totally different stories**.

You have individuals from three different layers experiencing the exact same situation in three completely different ways. **This is how you learn.** This is where you dissect the situation, understand what happened and figure out if anybody is skewing the story. From this you make your sound decision about where to go and how the situation should be handled.

If you are new at management – do not exclusively trust your OWN impression, from the outside. **Listen** to the people involved, **learn** and **then** make decisions. **Never** be afraid to make a decision. If it is positively wrong, you can change it and make another one. It is **not** embarrassing to back track if you were wrong the first time.

**Do not waste time holding on to a decision you <u>know</u> is wrong.**

Make another one. Quickly.

When you have encountered many of these situations, you can make decisions with only one or two of the parties involved - or may be none!  May be THEN you can make a decision just on your **own** experience, gathered over many years of managing.

As you will find throughout this book, I never use the expression:

I listened to my managers.

I <u>did</u> listen to my managers. However, there was **no need** to listen to them consistently.

**I already knew what they wanted.**

It can be summarized in just a few sentences, the content being self-evident:

Recruit a good team.
Make them as productive as possible, as quickly as possible with as few expenses as possible.
Create a safe work environment.
Create conditions which retains an employee as long as possible – **it is expensive to hire and train team members**.
Set attainable goals.
Drive the process to get to the goals.

Simply put:

Invest as little revenue as possible, but as much of yourself and your ingenuity as possible, for the largest attainable result. Follow the process closely, and have clear bench marks to know how you are doing.

# COMMUNICATION

Communication is the ultimate key to success. Without the ability to communicate effectively with your team about what you want to achieve – how can it be achieved?

To understand how extremely difficult communication can be I would like to refer to an instance where I was training ten team members over the course of a week. During one of the sessions I described a specific operation with three clear, distinct sentences. The meaning of the three sentences was – in my understanding – crystal clear.

One of the participants asked me if I meant something **entirely different**. So different, in fact, that I thought he could have misheard, or misunderstood me. When I asked him to explain, he said:

Well….didn't you say:

Then he **quoted** my three sentences, **word by word.**

So – from those three sentences, one team member out of ten had understood something **entirely different** than had the nine others, who understood the same as me. But his explanation was 100% reasonable – it was **indeed** possible to understand the three sentences the way **he** had interpreted them!

This indicates clearly the difficulties in communicating well, and how you have to **take great care in making**

**sure** that you are understood.

To avoid such misunderstandings, I got into the habit of explaining things from different angles – to rehash the same sentences chronologically different, all the while asking questions if everybody understood the sentences as I did.

**Repetition is the mother of learning.**

This is an extremely important element of communication. One of my Branch Manager's favorite expressions was:

× *We have really good people, so we only have to reiterate ten times.*

How true.

When you try to communicate with your team, all kinds of thoughts are going to each and every member's head. Some of the listeners will hear **one** part of a sentence, some will hear **other** parts of it. Some of them will remember **some** of the words as they relate to **them**, others will remember **other** words. Some of them will **remember the whole sentence**, as they find it important. Some of them will **totally forget about it**, because the **next** sentence seems more important.

**This is why** you can **never** allow yourself to be exasperated or irritated if your team either

Do not do what you say.
Do some of it.
Do something totally different.

They either –

Did not hear what you said.
Did not hear all of what you said.
Heard what you said, but did not quite understand some of it.
Heard what you said and understood it, but did not quite understand how to do it.
Heard what you said, understood it, started doing it, but did not know how to finish it.

Did you ever notice in school, how a math problem the teacher presented on the board seemed crystal clear to you? The method and solution appeared to be something **anybody** would understand and be able to do. Then the teacher said:

**Now you do it.**

And you could not. You could not repeat the procedure to save your life. What just minutes ago had seemed like the simplest problem in the world to solve had now become a locked box, a black, unsolvable mystery.

Sometimes, that is exactly how your team feels.

It is **YOUR** responsibility, as a teacher, coach and manager, to make sure that **your** team is functioning correctly according to **your** instructions. That is why -

**YOU** <u>always</u> **have to struggle to become a better communicator -**

and it starts with **repeating** what you said, over and over

again – in different ways, from different angles –
**while you are demonstrating how it is done.**

During my time as a Branch Manager in the United States I had a regional team who displayed the ultimate combination of communication and education over a 12 branch region from New Jersey to Washington, DC.

From this team of three managers, located in Philadelphia, there were **never** any delays in communicating **anything and everything** the branch managers needed to know. We had a conference call at least once a week with branch manager, service manager and office manager present in each office, a total of 39 people exchanging information.

The regional team was most of the time on the road and they would show up in the morning, unannounced, in different branches in the region. They would take over the computers for several hours and print management reports. They would **first** go through them and **then** review them with the managers in the office, making sure we understood exactly **what** the reports said, **how** they worked, and **how** to compare them.

The sales manager would later break out with the branch sales manager, the service manager with his counterpart in the branch, and the head of the region with the branch manager.

This was a **very** effective system of communication, management and education which ensured that **everybody** was **always** on the same page **moving forward with the same amount of information.**

**This** is the way to communicate – **frequent, hands on and one-on-one**. The region team was demanding, but always helpful, positive and goal oriented. They were incredibly knowledgeable and had an intense drive and enthusiasm which all of us were very much taken in by.

They functioned as **excellent role models** for how a management team ideally should work – and that is **exactly** what you should expect from a manager, or a management team:

**To be role models and lead by an example which you, as a junior manager, want to follow.**

# THE COMFORT ZONE

In talking to a manager in England, I made a statement that there were a lot of different opinions about management in America. His immediate answer was: "Yes - but it is best if they stay in America, though!"

Such a statement signifies a manager who has no interest in improving himself, his organization or his results. The only issue that concerns him is to conserve the status quo and the balance of power, by sticking his head in the sand to avoid changes. This manager's attitude to management is **very** common, and can be described as:

**"Do not step on my turf. I get scared and jealous. I do not want to hear about anything that can rock my world, which may force me to change, and do things differently."**

People **RESIST CHANGE** with every ounce of energy in their body. However – that is **the key** to improve your management:

**CHANGE**.

Humans like to stay in their comfort zone. They feel warm and fuzzy, confident, good about themselves, achieve things within their set borders – **but they do not develop!** If you want to be a successful manager, you **have to** get out of your comfort zone.

Put yourself out there and see what happens. May be you will float – may be you will sink. If you sink – work harder.

One thing is for sure, you will find out a lot about yourself and about other people. By doing that, **you cannot avoid** starting to develop. You can become good at things you never even thought you could approach - never in your wildest fantasy thought you would try. Suddenly you find yourself doing it, because you have just slid into it by pure necessity, because it **needs** to be done, it **needs** to happen. When it **needs** to happen – you **will** be doing it. **You have no choice**, so now you will learn it.

This is how you **force** yourself out of your comfort zone, and start developing into a **real** manager. Test yourself, and see what happens. Your comfort zone will get larger and larger. Soon you cannot remember what your comfort zone **used to be**, because you feel comfortable in **any** situation.

People often think they have to be born with abilities. They do not. What did Einstein say about being a genius?

**"It is 10% inspiration and 90% transpiration"**

which means – with serious intent and hard work, you can achieve virtually anything.

The bottom line is – and this is how you do **not** develop:

× *If you always do what you always did, you always get*

*what you always got.*

Is that how you want to be remembered as a manager?

When I called my Region Manager 15 years after I left the company we worked for, I had not spoken to him for all that time. He gave me a compliment I will forever cherish:

**.......yes, I remember you were good with the team.**

I was good with the team because I:

*LISTENED*

to the team members, and

*CHANGED*

what needed to be changed, to reach the goals we set.

It is **not** more complicated than that. It is actually **very simple**.

In short –

**1. Get out of your comfort zone.**
**2. Listen to your team members and your customers.**
**3. Make the necessary changes.**

While doing that you simultaneously **have to** make your team feel that they have an input, that **they are a crucial, integral part of the process** to get to the goal– **which they indeed are!**
They are **THE** crucial, integral part.

## PRESENCE AND RETENTION

Management is presence, both physically and mentally.

When I arrived in the United States from Norway, I told my Region Manager that at home I had four weeks' vacation during the summer, 10 days at Christmas, a week at Easter, several days off in the spring and 12 days of unauthorized sick leave. He calmly looked at me and said:

× *If I could do without you for that long, I could do without you altogether.*

Excellent point. How can you manage a team or an operation for twelve months by being absent two of them – almost 17% of the time? The answer is: **You cannot**. There is **no way** you can have a real continuity in managing a team with such lack of presence.

**You are** - de facto - **an unnecessary expense**.

Your presence is needed, demanded, required for your team to perform at its very best. There are no two ways about it.

Your attitude to presence in your team is <u>contagious.</u>

**Whatever you are, your team will perceive as <u>the way to be</u>**.

It has **got** to be **you**, first and foremost, leading the way –

**then** the team will follow.

The attitude to presence is very much changeable. Mine was. From having all that time off in Norway, I came to a situation where I had 6 paid holidays a year and earned 1 week vacation after 1 year and 2 weeks after two years. My attitude **changed radically**. From having a total of about 6 weeks off and using all my sick days every year in Norway– I was not off sick **one single day** the first 9 years working in the U.S.A. The feeling of achievement in being able to spend every day continuously working and creating a well performing team was immense. But you **cannot** be away. It is **you, you,** and **only you** doing it. Your team needs to feel that you are **always** available, in **some way.**

Your presence also needs to be felt by your external customers. They need to know you are **always** there, **always** prepared and ready to help sorting out potential problems. **Never, ever** forget who PAY YOUR WAGES.

**Your external customers**.

They **have to** be able to feel your personal presence.

Presence is also power. If anything in management is power, it is presence. Management is not about **demonstrating power**, but about **demonstrating presence.** You will gain **more** power the **more** you are present. It cannot be ignored that you are actually **there**, where it happens, and not in some faraway office.

So - presence is power - **good power** - but it is also **the key to retention**, and **RETENTION** is the most important factor in a company's dynamics. **The** most important factor. Retention - as in retaining **both** your internal **and** your external customers – is the key to a company's survival and growth.

Record breaking sales are good – but what does it matter if there is **no** retention from the sales – **no** recurring revenue? What does it matter if a large company sells $ 40 million in service work, if they are sued for $ 30 million and have cancellations of already existing, renewable policies for $ 10 million? (These are real numbers from real companies). This is called **spinning wheels**, and doing the service becomes an exercise for the sake of exercising.

What if the company sold **nothing**, but **retained** the $ 40 million? It would be **much** better off, because to anything the company sold **next** year, you could add the retained $ 40 million from this year. There would be **no** erosion of the customer base, even if there were **no** sales, which means you still have work enough to keep your team stable, and you are ready for more influx of revenue.

If you have **no** sales **and** loss – now you **really** have to start to look around and wonder what to do with your team.

Do you have to let some of them go, because of lack of work?
If so, what do you do when the situation changes and revenue starts to flow in?
Do you start over?
Do you take on the costly and time consuming job of training members of a new team?
You have **no choice** but to do so, and that is **not** a good situation to get into.

**Retention is the key to stability.**

To **grow**, you have to **retain** – both internal and external customers.
To **retain** customers you have to **do good service**.
To **do good service** you have to have **a team who wants to** do good service.
To make the **team want to do good service** –

<u>YOU</u> **have to show them why they should.**

<u>**Your team needs your presence**</u>

**both** in the field **and** in the office, as a confirmation that you are behind their efforts, the company is behind their efforts, and **they are doing the right things to retain your customers**.

<u>**Your customers need your presence**</u>

to be reassured that **everything is stable** and the resources are available in case they should need them, and they know who to relate to:

**YOU.**

<u>**Remember:**</u>

**People resist change**. Your internal and external customers are no different. Your presence confirms that **everything is stable**, **nothing changes,** and they can stay firmly embedded in their comfort zone.

**That** is how both groups are retained, and **it all comes**

**down to YOU, and how you manage it.**

# IMPRESSING THE TEAM

How do you make an impression on your team?

## BY BEING YOU.

There is no other way of doing it, as you can be nobody else. **Do not** try to be somebody or something you are not. The moment a seed is sown in the mind of your team that you are not genuine, **they lose confidence in you**.

There is an expression saying -

× *there are too many chiefs and not enough Indians.*

However, if **you** can be **a real Indian chief** – **that** is the way to manage. Indian chiefs -

were **not** put into power.
They were **not** elected.
They had **no** military rank.
They could **not rise** through the organization to **become** a chief.

The warriors simply followed -

**the chief who impressed them the most**.

The one that had most success in war.
The one that lived up to their expectations.
The one they truly felt could lead them to success.

**If you can be a true Indian chief – you will be successful.**

You have two specific tools at your disposal:

**To be you.**
**Doing the right things.**

If you do the right things -

**YOU become the good culture of your team.**

Here are some of the keys to create a good culture:

<u>Always be on time</u>

× *If you are not early, you are late.*

Very true.

Nobody manages to come dead on the very second eight o'clock. So be a bit early, and never be late. **NEVER BE LATE.**

<u>You</u> **are the one setting the tone. If** <u>you</u> **can be late,** <u>everybody</u> **can be late.**

During my time as a student at a Norwegian university, lateness was embedded in the academic culture. It was accepted that the students could be up to 15minutes late for the lectures. The teachers would be waiting, through something he called "the academic quarter". At an institution teaching a curriculum of the highest education you can achieve in the Norwegian society, the university's leadership was simultaneously infusing lateness as a way of life into future business leaders. It was a **complete reversal** of the process of how to become effective and productive. It was absolutely and completely unacceptable. You **cannot** manage anything with a calendar built on the acceptance of lateness - but that was what the university taught us.

Never demonstrate power or claim privileges.

During a working visit to an insurance company, I had the doubtful pleasure of seeing a senior manager keeping court surrounded by his "inferiors", demonstrating everything a manager should never, ever do. He had gathered a team of 6 or 8 members, in the middle of the afternoon, when everybody should have been busy working. To my surprise I spotted him by a long desk, surrounded by the team with his legs crossed and solidly planted on the table, reading a newspaper. Laughing loudly he clearly demonstrated that he was the only one who was allowed do this, and the team members chatted to him and laughed subserviently as they found appropriate, to appease the powerful guru. This is **NOT** the way to manage.

Not only did he demonstrate all the things you should never do – he enforced his power by showing that he was the only one allowed to do it. He likewise demonstrated the negative principle of

× *do what I say, not what I do.*

It was unthinkable for any of his "inferiors" to put **their** feet on the table, **for them** to read a paper during working hours and **for them** to be **loud and obnoxious**.

You do not have to **demonstrate** your power.

**You are already in possession of it**.

Everybody knows it. To also **demonstrate it** will turn your team members off.

There is absolutely **no reason whatsoever** for members of a team to be committed to such a manager, and the **destruction** he causes to the company culture is **incalculable**.

The only reason why team members will accept such a manager is because they think the correct culture is to manage up. **It is not**.

**You have to manage down, in order to improve your people.**

If you do, **you do not have to** manage up – that will take care of itself when your capability becomes self-evident in the success of you operation.

**Manage up, by managing down!**

# FATAL PITFALLS.
# HOW TO LOSE YOUR TEAM'S CONFIDENCE.

**People want and need stability.**

You have to be calm.
Cool.
Composed.
Level headed.
Even tempered.
Decided.

Your team does not want to face a **different** person, in the **same** body, every day of the week.

Your plans need to be clearly defined  and not presented before they are. Never appear undecided.

One of my managers would openly discuss with one of his team - and in everybody's presence - how he aimed to manage the next few, troublesome days. He went through six different possible scenarios in shorter time than it takes to write this paragraph. The team knew that none of the plans would come true, as they all involved him getting up at 5:00 in the morning. He was always late – up to 1.5 hours. None of the six scenarios ever materialized.

Needless to say, he could never become a respected manager, as he was already written off as laughing stock.

When your plans are clear – stick to them!

Any member of your team who perceives that he or she works towards a specific goal, which then suddenly changes or disappears - stops working.

**There is nothing to work _towards_!**

Work becomes "going through the motions", and that must never be allowed to happen. If you see this happening,

**gather your team, reintroduce the goal and confirm your commitment to it**.

When you introduce a goal and the path to get there -

There will be those who follow with great eagerness.
There will be those who want to follow but cannot. They need your help.
There will be those who will be "hangers on" for the praise of reaching the goal. Give them tasks to do, to help them reach it. If they do not do the tasks – leave them behind.
There will be those who will object to go with you. Leave them behind at the start.

Always do what you say you are going to do.

A promise has to be iron clad. If you say "I will come out and work with you today" – barring a death in your family, you **HAVE TO** go. The demonstration of lack of support in **not** doing that is an **extremely strong statement**, telling your team that they can be ignored at any time, for any reason. And then….

**they will ignore you.**

You can never say – "I intended to do it, but something came up".

*×The road to Hell is paved with good intentions!*

**Always** do what you say you are going to do.

Never blackmail your team.

A manager hired me for a specific job at a high rate of pay. However, he told me that if I did not work all the days I committed to, which was 21, he would reduce my high hourly rate with two thirds. After 7 days I was uncere-moniously told that the job was done, and the **3 week**, high paying job I was blackmailed into, became only **1 week**.

Needless to say, this manager would struggle hard to find a team who would be committed to him.

Always treat everybody equally, and as equals.

Everybody **MUST** be treated equally. Even a hint of pre-ferential treatment will make the most close-knit team unravel instantly – and you will never be able to repair it. It is simply irreparable.

**Even** if you extend yourself to the **uttermost** to avoid pre-ferential treatment to anybody in your team – you will still **more than likely** be accused of it. Talk to the member who feels that preferential treatment has been extended, and clear the air on the subject. Never let it fester – it will break up your team and undermine your organization. All your invested time and effort in building a cohesive team will amount to nothing.

<u>Take action on wrongdoing.</u>

If you want to preserve the team's faith in you, take immediate action on wrongdoing.

You can **only** get commitment from a team if you are **fair** in your judgement and **swift** in your actions – both inwards in the team, and outwards.

On one occasion I had a team member who came into the office and loudly harassed the customer service representatives, person by person for his dissatisfaction with schedules and their work in general. If you allow that to pass, you lose your team's faith in you, and hence **your power**. The customer service representatives may do certain kinds of work in certain kinds of ways, but **YOU** have told them how and when to do it. The result of it is **YOUR** responsebility, so whoever is dissatisfied with how the operation works needs to come to **YOU.**

Everybody is now looking at **YOU**. What is going to happen? The damage inward in the team is severe, irreparable. It will be festering resentment between the team members, something that will inhibit the effectiveness of your operation dramatically. You cannot afford it and you cannot allow it to happen.

In this particular incident, I let the offender go, immediately. That restored the closeness of the team and cemented the commitment to the manager and the direction of the team's effort.

On occasion I have had calls from external customers who have made severe complaints against team members – hit-

and-run, theft etc.

**Always stand by your team while finding out what happened.**

Never be judgmental or show emotional bias before you know relevant facts. Clearly your team members deserve the benefit of the doubt. **You** picked them! Go on an intensive fact finding mission with both the customer and the team, and if you know your team, a quick conversation will most often establish the facts about the situation.

You have put **a lot of time and effort** into each member of the team. If you show as much as a hint of distrust in any of them, they will never be a fully committed member of your team, ever again. Do not destroy your hard work needlessly. If the accusation eventually shows to be true, then deal with it accordingly.

Always make sure that you do all the necessary preparations for a timely pay.

People work for money. Make no mistake about it. Weather it is incentives, commissions, bonuses or regular pay it **HAS** to be on time. If not, your team's faith in you will immediately evaporate. Their attitude will be -

"We always do everything on time to get things done for the best of the team – and the manager cannot even pay us correctly, and on time?"

Appreciation makes people feel really good about themselves. Praise is great.

**But their kids cannot eat it.**

<u>Never expect more from anybody else, than you expect from yourself.</u>

To expect something different from your team than from yourself is an extremely strong negative statement.

**Do not** expect your team to do something **you** would not do.

If **you** will not do it - **do not** make anybody else do it. Listen to the concerns voiced by your team. If a member clearly states:

I am apprehensive about this –

find out why, and address it. May be it can be solved, if not, **DO NOT** force anybody into doing something they are apprehensive about. Nothing good can come out of it.

If you think the apprehension is *unreasonable* - revisit the hiring process and find out if you and the team member have to re-evaluate the employment.

On the flip side:

**Never do anything you would not allow your staff to do.**

**<u>Do not keep privileges to yourself.</u>**

# YOU ARE THE CULTURE

When you are the manager,

**<u>you</u> are the culture**.

People are led by example - the attitude **you** project will be the attitude throughout **your** team. I have experienced corporate cultures where both managers and employees in a humorous way promoted the absence of work ethic.

It was expressed through the greeting process:

"How are you today?"
"It's Monday" – *a negative*. I have the whole week ahead of me, and it's awful.
"How are you today?"
"It's Wednesday" – *a semi-positive*. I am closer to the week end.
"How are you today?"
"It's Friday" – *a positive*. It's great! It's the day before the week end.
"How are you today?"
"It's just two hours" (to home time) - *a positive*. I will be out of here soon, and I can't wait.
"Are you OK?"
"I **will** be in about 3 hours" (going home).

The attitudes expressed clearly states an idealism of doing as little as possible for as short a time as possible and then go home.

This indicates a corporate culture where it appears to be a total disconnect between managers and the people they manage. Such a culture grows out of the lack of management involvement in the teams – to act as leaders, define goals and set bench mark to reach those goals -

**and personally oversee the process**.

It gives the impression that the employees are left to themselves to find the way, with no real opportunity to impact events, and the only way they will find – because it is the only way which seems attractive – is **the way home.**

You may say that the attitude described above illustrates the European quest for the shortest possible work week and as much time off as possible. Regrettably, it is poorly understood by the people living in such a culture that -

**when the actual cultural DRIVE is to work less and less, the whole society suffers. It becomes an approved attitude that nobody cares,**

because -

do we **REALLY** care about the results of the things we do if it is a Friday afternoon and we are going fishing? The cultural drive is to **get away**, and **not to do more than we absolutely have to**.

We **should** care – but **why** should we care?

We should care because **our manager has shown us** why we should.

He works 60 hours a week.
He gets things done.
His operation is improving at record speed.
His sales force is better than any other sales force.
He is successful, and he makes money.

Would you not like to do the same?

**That is what managers do.**

And hence he also knows that

× *the more you do, the more you get done.*

There is no doubt about it. I have had jobs where I could barely stop to breathe and it made me extremely effective. I had to make decisions – **then and there**. Get it done. Get on with it and go to the next task.

I have had periods with oceans of time, where I could get nothing done in 3 days, other than wondering what to do, but not to start on anything major, in fear of taking on too much to cope with. It is a **very dangerous** situation to get into. I got **extremely** ineffective and unproductive.

However - this tells you something very interesting and exiting – something showing how **YOU** can be both a creative and a deciding force within a group of people:

**One** person can serve as the home of **several different** working personalities -

The **culture around** that person and **the pressure he or she is under**, partially decides **who** that person is.

Somebody who may appear to be **extremely lazy** in one team can in a **different** team suddenly be **extremely productive**.

This is where the manager comes in**:**

**It is YOUR TASK to create the environment and the challenges necessary to bring out the effective and productive personality in a person.**

**You** are the trendsetter. **You** are the guiding light. In short

<u>you</u> are **THE LEADER**.

Whatever you do, whatever you set into motion and whatever you enforce, will be the result of your organization.

<u>You have to be in tune with and keep track of your team at any given time.</u>

If you ask a manager:

"Where is your team, and what are they doing right now?" and he or she says:
"I am not quite sure"

– he or she is **not** managing the team. How can you manage your team when you do not know where they are, or what they are doing?

**"I think they went over to Johnson to look at a problem".**

You think? You cannot **think** where your team is, or what

they are up to. You **GOT** to **KNOW**, **always**. How can you adjust your operation from hour to hour if you do not know where your team is, and what they are doing -

**AT ANY GIVEN TIME**?

**You HAVE TO know.**

That is the only way to operate effectively, or else –

× *the inmates are running the asylum.*

When you want to find out exactly how your team operates, you have to physically **inspect** your customers' premises **and** communicate with your team members about the **same** premises, **to correlate what you see with what you hear**.

Make sure that what you want to happen is actually happening. You expect the service to be done in certain ways **and** the customers' premises to be at a certain state

× *Inspect what you expect.*

<u>**Inspect to confirm that it is.**</u>

## CUSTOMER SERVICE - EXTERNAL

I have previously spoken about responsibility, and that it is all yours. Responsibility means that **you are the company**, and the company is **you**.

**You** are **the manager** of the company, which means that **you** deal with trouble. That is what management is.

**You are the manager of trouble**.

If there was no trouble – what would there be to manage? You do not have to manage something that is no trouble. It manages itself.

You learn to manage trouble **in the field**. It cannot be learned behind a desk.

**Good and successful managers are created face to face with potential and existing customers, <u>in the field</u>.**

**NOT IN THE OFFICE!**

To be able to manage well you **have to get out**, communicate with your customers and show a presence for your team. How can you manage a team if you do not know first-hand what they are facing, and only rely on verbal feedback? You **have to** be there, to **see for yourself**.

This is how you **earn your team's respect**. It is what gives you **power to decide the direction** within the team.

It is also how you **earn your customers' respect.** Simultaneously you create a database in your brain to compare incoming information about similar situations later.

<u>It is easiest to face difficult situations with no preconceived notions.</u>

If a customer calls up with a complaint of a more serious matter – you have to go there and see what is going on. I used to have preconceived notions. I made up potential scenarios and created solutions as to how to fix them, before even going to customers' locations. My manager taught me a simple way how to avoid those preconceived notions. When I expressed my concerns, he simply said:

× *Just go there. The most important thing is to show up. It shows that you care. What you are worrying about may not even come up!*

He was right. The customer was extremely pleased that somebody showed up. What I feared would come up, was not even an issue.

So - never fear going out, however bad the situation may seem. **Never fear**. Remember –

× *Today is the first day in the rest of your life.*

Go ahead and live it. Good experiences teach you nothing. *Nothing*. It is from the **bad** experiences you learn. But what makes you **successful**, is -

**to turn bad experiences into good.**

To solve a problem.
To take care of a situation.
To satisfy your customer.
To support your team member, who is between the rock and the hard place.

**That** is how you **grow** and learn how to become a **real manager**. To do that, you **have to** go to where the action is, and **be present**.

Remember –

× *perception is reality*,

so **your most important tools** when going out in the field to face **any** situation are **your ears.**

**Listen** to what the customer has to say!

It may sound totally unreasonable to you, but **that is irrelevant – this** is how the customer **perceives** the situation and **you have to try** to understand it and see it the same way, **or** understand **how** it could be seen that way. Unless you do, you will **not** be able to help, and the customer and you might as well have been talking different languages.

If the customer's wish is something you can take care of **without** having to understand it – so much easier. You do not **have** to see eye to eye on the subject – the **only** thing that needs to happen is that **the customer gets his or her wish come true.** You do **not need** to understand the philosophy behind it, if it is something very simple which can be done then and there.

**Just do it! – and make the customer happy.**

Situations may turn bad, and sometimes they do. I have had exasperated, frustrated customers screaming in my face from two feet away, several times. Cry and scream that they are going to sue us, and **you just wait!** But it was because I was **the company**. They did not actually scream at **ME**. They screamed at **the manager of the company**.

This is where you learn to keep your cool. Your cool is paramount while being **the manager.**

Never lose your cool.
It does not help.
It does not change anything.
It does not make anything better.
So you might as well keep it.
Your cool.

**And** you have to be professional.
**And** you have to be polite.
**And** you have to be patient.

Frustrated customers are allowed to be as frustrated as they want. Their **perception** is that they have paid for something, and they have not gotten it. Something in their world has gone horribly wrong! Their hard earned money seems to have been completely wasted, and it is for **you** to sort it out. **You** are the manager of the company, so **you** need to keep your cool - to calm the customer down, **and** deal with the trouble.

Do not display a massive array of damage control, making it even more confusing and frustrating for the customer.

Do not suggest anything.
Do not tell the customer what he or she ought to do.
Do not tell them what **you** can do.

The solution is **simple**, it is close at hand, **easy** and the most natural thing in the world. It just takes **one** question to get started, and the whole process will run unaided. The question is:

**What would you like to see happen?**

The customer will tell you. Then you can go from there. Wherever it leads. Just know your limitations.

You know what **you** can do, then and there. What can **the company** do? Find out. Go on the phone and find out.

May be the company can do what the customer wants. May be it cannot. You are the manager and the messenger, with a quadruple function:

**To find out the facts about what happened, what went wrong, or what the customer <u>feels</u> went wrong.**

**To do, personally, whatever is necessary to appease and satisfy the customer.**

**Not to promise something that cannot be done, neither by you, nor the company.**

**To find out what the company can do, to resolve the issue.**

**THAT IS IT.**

There is nothing more to it. **You** took responsibility and **you** solved the problem to the extent it could be solved, by **anybody**.

Time is you enemy.

In all customer relations, time is your biggest enemy. The modern phones have solved this problem completely. 40 years ago you had to get to a phone, either in your office or a pay phone on the street. That took away the advantage of being prompt in customer relations.

When a customer calls, they want **response.**
They do not expect the impossible, **even** if they will tell you so.

**They want a response.**

They **do not want to be ignored**, and they know for a fact that you can reach them within seconds.

**Respond immediately. Immediately.**

Pick up your phone and call! If the customer is not available – leave a message and **follow up**. Call again. **Soon.** It is **your** task to follow up and make sure you get in contact with the customer. **YOUR task**. **Not** the customer's. If you do not follow up, you will quickly be back to the situation **before** the customer called the first time.

**Your response** will take almost all the urgency out of the customer's request. The customer now feels that the matter is settled– it has been brought to a manager's attention, it is scheduled to be taken care of.

**The customer can fall back into his or her comfort zone.**

Instead of making a **new** problem by **not** responding, you have already taken care of **most** of the original problem – **just by responding**.

# AGE

How old are you when you become a good manager?

**There is no way to tell.**

What you know for a fact is that it takes field experience, facing –

Potential customers.
Existing customers.
Previous customers.
Smiling customers.
Angry customers.
Hostile customers.
Deceiving customers.
Small problems.
Large problems.
Odd problems.
Good solutions to problems.
Bad solutions to problems.
Good employees.
Difficult employees.
Motivated employees.
Employees with no motivation.
Accidents.
Injuries.
Long days.
Long nights.
Long working week-ends.
Lack of sleep.

Frustration.
Fatigue.............

The list is **endless.** It tells you that a truly good manager is probably **not** 20 years old. But at 20, you can certainly have a **good potential** – you just have to **apply everything you are and the skills you have**, to **become** a good manager.

It is truly rewarding to watch good managers do what they do. They serve as role models, they inspire you, enlighten you and they make you want to be like them. But in order to be like them – you **cannot** just watch them. You are **not** going to become a good manager by osmosis – by transferring skills from them to you during some psychological event which over time will turn **you** into **them**.

It is **all** up to **you**!

**You need to take a look at that list.**

**When are you starting on it**?

At 20 years of age? 25? 30?

You **do not** have to be in a management position to start on it. You can start at **any time**. As a matter of fact, it is easier to start the learning process at a **lower level** in the hierarchy, as you normally **face customer much more frequently** – on a daily basis – than do office based managers.

Can a 35 year old manager be better at management than a 50 year old manager?

**Absolutely.**

It all depends on **real experience**. Not how long you have been a manager. Real experience facing tasks and problems in need of solutions.

To watch another manager for 10 years and then move into his or her chair at the office does not automatically make you a good manager - not necessarily even as good as the previous one.

You learn very little by **watching** something.
You have to **do** it.

**YOU** have to do it.

By exposing yourself to any and all situations which could possibly arise in the position you are in, you learn to become a manager **through a process you sometimes are not even aware of**.

Opinions and attitudes are shaped in our mind based on the experience you gather by **putting yourself on the firing line.** Often you will find yourself making statements and orchestrate solutions **without even thinking – good solutions** stemming from combinations of what you have read, heard - and seen in the field.

**Good solutions you could not have dreamed up just a few years earlier now seem crystal clear and self evident to you**.

**This is how you become a manager**, and it does **not** necessarily have to do with age.

# EUROPEAN AND AMERICAN PARADIGMS IN EXCELLENT CUSTOMER SERVICE

Customer service means vastly different things to different people. Most Norwegians and Brits would not recognize good customer service if they experienced it – my distinct impression is that they would not quite understand what they were looking at. Most Americans would be appalled by the lack of it, if they visited Norway or Great Britain.

I had to undergo **a massive paradigm shift** when managing businesses in the USA. The demand from American customers was infinitely higher - **"it has to happen right here and right now"** - a concept unheard of when coming from Norway. As I was accustomed to Norwegian customer service, or lack of same – I could not understand **how** such service could be expected. When I broke through into the American paradigm – suddenly I **could not see why** it could **not** be expected**.**

American customers demand **instant satisfaction** because they **can** - because of the intense competition. It is easy to see how this comes about. In Baltimore, Maryland in the Washington Metropolitan area - a city with only about 1.4 million inhabitants - there are more than 100 pest control companies.

You have to become **a manager of instant satisfaction**. It is not difficult – it just demands certain **planned strategies** involving **priority** and **time**, but it **will** require some of the elements I touched on in the first chapter:

**Forget about regular routines in your life.**
**Forget about coming home to dinner at the same time every day.**
**Forget about regular holidays.**
**Forget about the books telling you that you can be so organized that you can put a week's worth of work into a 9 hour work day.**

A few illustrations will highlight the stark contrast between the expectations of customer service in the different environments:

A **Tuesday** morning during a large job in Delaware I needed some equipment which at the time I could not find in the U.S. I called a company in England stating what I needed and that I **had to** have it by **Friday**, as I had a crew working through the week end. The answer was:

**No problem.**

I paid about $ 2 000 upfront and waited for Friday.

Friday – and the week end - came and went, no equipment arrived, and the crew was sitting **paid**, but **empty handed**.

A phone call Monday morning revealed that "the equipment was in Liverpool, ready to be shipped." Needless to say I cancelled the purchase, and during the day I finally found a company in Chicago carrying similar equipment, if not exactly the same. **They sent it overnight**.

When the telephone rings in the United States, you **have to** pick it up no later than on the third ring. **You have to.** If not, your existing customer will think that something is wrong with the line or there is nobody in the office. If you pick it up on the fourth ring, and it is a potential new customer, he or she will already have hung up and gone to the next company on the list.

If it is an existing customer in need of service – the **only way** it is **not** going to be today, is if **they** cannot do it today. If **they** can, **you** have to do it **the same day**.

If a piece of equipment with a warranty breaks down in the U.S., you will have another one brought out to you that day, while yours is taken back for repairs. To be without the equipment, and **lose a whole day of production is unthinkable**.

In England a piece of equipment under warranty broke down. After two days the company carrying the equipment showed up, and said what we **could** have done was to have **our own** engineering department take look at it! **A week later** I got a similar piece of equipment on loan and upon enquiring about when I could have my own back – the answer was:

**In two months**.

In two months the Apollo space craft of 1969 could have made 10 return trips around the moon. The current New Horizon Probe – which just passed Jupiter after 9 years of space travel - could have done 180 return trips. Still, within England, **two months** is needed to take a piece of equipment back to the shop, fix it and bring it back?

The purpose of comparing these scenarios is that it **clearly** shows:

With modern communication – cars, trains, planes, carrier services, shipping services, telephones, computers, e-mail, texting, GPS – or Sat Nav –

Managing a business **expediently** is entirely possible. **Entirely possible.**

**<u>WHY</u> would not customer service be virtually instant?**

**So why does it not happen?**

There can only be **one** answer:

**<u>No manager in charge and lack of proper management,</u>**

and there is **no** feeling of urgency among the managers who **should be** in charge. **None.** As a matter of fact there is a factor present which I call

**"The Resistance Factor"**

The managers are **well entrenched in their comfort zones** and they **intensely resist** to move out of it.

**People resist change with every ounce of energy in their body!**

The resistance factor can be easily illustrated by an experience I had after arriving in the U.S., when my Region Manager informed me that a customer needed a manager immediately, and to please make contact. I asked: "Now?" - upon which he replied: "The phone is right next to your hand. Pick it up".

× *The one who picks up the phone first, wins!*

Indeed. **Why delay it? Why** make a customer dissatisfied by having to pick up the phone **again**? Instantly I had displayed my resistance factor. Instead of jumping on it I was hesitating, resisting.

If the customers **do not expect anything better** than what they already have – the situation will stay at a status quo - **no development** of excellent managers.

× *If you always do what you always did, you always get what you always got!*

The change in attitude to expedient service was **not** the only paradigm shift I had to go through. It also very much involved the concept that doing good customer service **does not** make you subservient. In Europe I felt that a full commitment to serving others made you subservient.

**Nothing** could be further from the truth!

You are not actually **serving** customers, you are **servicing their premises.** You are **helping** them. Helping them with issues they cannot manage themselves –

Issues creating barriers, inhibiting their lives - barriers **you** can remove.
Things they are afraid of, but you are not, which **you** can take care of to ease their fears.
Tasks they are incapable of doing themselves, but **you** can do, and hence they can get them done.

**You** become a **helping friend**, highly appreciated if you can solve problems they cannot.

**<u>That</u> is what customer service is.**

When you **know** that, and you fully adapt it as your paradigm of excellent customer service, it is –

Easy to be positive.
Easy to be helpful.
Easy to go the extra mile.
Easy to extend yourself in ways you never thought possible **before** adapting the paradigm.

And since your customers in addition are willing to **pay you** for the privilege, you should be **happy** they picked **you,** and nobody else!

# PERFORMANCE REVIEWS

Performance reviews. They are very important parts of the fact finding mission for your management strategy.

If you have close contact with your team members, performance reviews should not give you any surprises – but still they do. Issues are revealed that you did not know were issues, and they are happening **every day, right under your nose**.

A performance review is often seen as a short session with your manager where he tells you how you are doing. Have **you** ever had a performance review done with **your** manager? He arrives with a two page document with boxes to check and a dotted line for you to sign on. It is clearly a task which is **down prioritized**, but something that has to be done once a year. Everything is fine...do you have any questions?....sign here. See you in twelve months.

This is **not** a performance review. At best, it is an exercise to keep a paper trail telling the upper management that something was done. However – a performance review, it was **not**.

A performance review should more correctly be called a **performance re-interview**. It is a situation where you, the manager, have a change to **re-interview** your team member. **You** are not telling **them** how they are doing. They already know that, **if** you have communicated with them continuously every day, every week and every moth throughout the year, as you should. This is where **you** have a chance **to find out more about them**. It is **your** opportunity to ask open ended questions to have **them** tell **you**, in their own words, what their world looks like working for you and the company. This is where you gather a lot of the information you need to adjust and correct your management strategy to get the optimal results out of **your investment**:

**Your team members**,

who you have invested all your time and effort in, for the highest possible return, through -

closeness of the team,
effectiveness of their work and
growth and retention of the customer base.

Reviews are often done on an annual basis. This is in my opinion **way** too infrequent, but in the hustle and bustle of everyday business, that is how it works.

The re-interview should be held in a psychologically neutral setting, and in a relaxed atmosphere. Your team members should **not** feel that they are dragged into your office in front of an annual tribunal. They will automatically shut down, and you will **not** get any information out of them. **You** as a **person** are powerful enough to encounter. **You, in your office, on your turf** – that is overwhelming.

Pick a place where they are comfortable, where they have been before in a different setting and where they feel relaxed enough to open up and talk - a meeting room where general meetings in the company are held etc. An even more relaxed atmosphere is in a fast food place, outside of the busy hours. If you know such a place, and you are at a stage where you are experienced enough to conduct it there without being side tracked - go for it.

Do not line up reviews on the clock in such a way that each team member knows he or she is on a conveyer belt moving towards the end of the conversation, and they only have so much time. You will **not** get any information from them – at least none other than the one which has been festering as negative I their mind for some time.

Have a clear strategy for where you want the review to go, just like an interview. You want to review **both** how the team member is performing in the job, **and**

**how he or she feels <u>about</u> the job.**

This is of paramount importance. Does he or she feel comfortable –

With you?
With the rest of the team?
In the office?
In the field?
At the customers?
With the vehicle.
With their equipment?
With the uniform?
With their compensation package?

Now I will introduce an issue of uttermost importance, which is partially or wholly ignored during reviews:

**How do they feel about their private life**?

This does not mean that you should probe into their private lives. It means that you should ask, out of concern, if there is anything **you** can do to iron out friction between their home life and work.

**It can be very simple issues.**

A field representative may want to start work one hour later, and work one hour later in the afternoon. Why not? **If it makes your team function better** – the employee will now be servicing the customers every day without a thorn in his or her side about this tiny time warp creating havoc in the home schedules. With the mind at ease and **off that issue**, he or she is going to function infinitely better in a customer service setting.

Make them talk. **Do not** lead the conversation – **initiate it**, and let **them** talk, and **LISTEN** to what they say. This is how you learn what is going through their minds, what they enjoy, what they dislike, what occupies them during the day, what is creating problems for them during that day and what lasting impressions they take home, influencing their private life – **and hence their attitude to work**. Do they curse work after they come home – or do they find it fulfilling and want to go back and do it again tomorrow?

It is **your** task and **your** responsibility to do **everything** in your power to push their impression along that gradient – **from negative towards positive**, and you do that by finding out what the members of your team think, feel and how they act. How do they perceive the world around them and how they respond to it? - because whatever they feel, the customer will notice – so the feeling better be **good!**

Then you create a strategy utilizing what you know about each team member to find a way to apply their abilities in the daily work to the ultimate result for both them and you.

No team is uniform. Each member has strong sides and weak sides. Some of them may have so many weak sides, you sometimes wonder if they are going to make it. These could be members that you did not hire. They were there when you came and so far have, in some way, functioned.

Take a look at their work ethic. Are these members doing their very best, but already working up to the maximum of their potential? If they are **functioning** and the customers are **satisfied** - support them and help them to be the best they can be - tolerate that they continue to perform at the standard they do **and** help them improve. Not everybody has to be as good as **you**. Not everybody has to be at the top of the team.

**They have to function satisfactorily in the job they are doing.**

If they do, why dismantle their effort because it is not up to **your** level?

× *Do not fix what is not broken.*

A very good example here is an old field representative, working in pest control all his life, but never educated very well throughout his working career – something **obviously** not his fault. He was famous for "not being able to kill a mouse if he stepped on one".

However, he managed a customer portfolio consisting of a single account worth $ 50 000 a year and I was told that if I took him off and supplied another member of my team - technically more adept - they would instantly cancel, with the statement:

**"Because we love him. Love him, love him, love him - and we don't care if we see a mouse".**

This case tells you **a lot** about customer service. Customer service is all about **making the customer happy.** You can be the best problem solver in the world – if he customer does not like you because you are **not open, communicative and service minded,** he or she is **not** going to be happy, no matter what you do and how good you are.

These are issues you have to focus on during reviews. Be flexible. Do not hold everybody to the same standard **technically** – take a look at their **functionality** in your team – but hold everybody to the same standard regarding **customer service**.

That **has** to be **iron clad**.

From your point of view, the performance review is a fact finding mission, making it possible to reveal the technical aspect and the customer service aspect of your team members, and how they are fused together in each and every one of them. Find areas to work on, make specific plans and schedule time to carry it out in the near future. In addition you need to find out how the team members function with each other, within the company and if there are home-workplace-issues that need to be handled.

For the team members it is extremely important to walk away with a confident feeling, of that they -

Understood everything during the meeting.
Know exactly where they stand regarding their performance as it relates to company standards.
What you think about their effort.
What you expect from them.

**There can be no uncertainty in the minds of your team members about these four issues**.

If it is, the team will be floundering, not knowing if they are to continue on what they are doing or to change course. Hence they will take random stabs at procedures instead of following the trail you want to blaze.

## DISCIPLINARY PROCEDURES

Managers shy away from disciplinary procedures. Sadly, the issue is well embedded as one of the responsibilities of management. Here is the good news:

**It is not difficult!**

The main reason why most managers – and most people – shy away from disciplinary action is that they perceive it as confrontational. Human beings do **not** like confrontation. They desperately avoid confrontation until they are pushed **so far**, they see no other option. Then they will emotionally lash out. Sometimes the apprehension is age related. A 30 year old manager may feel it inappropriate to discipline a 60 year old team member, as in his world growing up it was regularly done the other way around. Older people disciplined youngsters, not vice versa.

We hesitate to get into disciplinary actions because it appears to us that the situation of confrontation, emotions running high and lashing out does not seem compatible with a comfortable work environment. This is very true.

**It does not** – but then again, that is **not** how disciplinary actions come about. Disciplinary actions have **nothing** to do with confrontation **whatsoever**.

The process starts very simply with a well prepared, mutually agreed upon employment relationship. The **agreement** is between the **team member** and **you**, as a representative of the company. **You** know exactly what the job entails, what needs to be done, how and when. **Everything** has to be laid out in detail – the work hours, reporting in and out, how to do the job, what to use, safety precautions required, vehicle policy, reimbursement policy, notification to be off, paid holidays, vacation…..in short:

**There has to be a crystal clear understanding between you and the new team member about everything pertaining to the job – and it has to be drawn up on paper and signed by both.**

From the moment that document is signed, there will be no confrontation. The **only** thing **you** have to make sure of is that the team adheres to the policies.

It is **not** confrontational to take one of the team members into your office after work and simply say –

"I noticed you did this or that yesterday. I am sure you are aware that, according to our agreement about how the job is performed, that is not a part of the deal, and cannot be repeated."

That is simple information, **reiterating you previous agreement**. There is **nothing** confrontational in that and you do not in any way have to use body language, voice or facial expressions indicating emotional involvement. This is not an angry parent correcting a child, it is two adults exchanging information on a professional level. The employee may even have a **good reason** why he or she acts in the way you observe, but –

**it is not for you to question that reason – just to point**

out the fact that the behavior is not compatible with the job description. <u>That</u> is your job, <u>but that is also all it is.</u>

If it goes any further, run through a certain progressive sequence of warnings laid out in the job description, so the team member **at any given time** knows where he or she stands. It may be verbal warning first and then written warnings. If there is a law pertaining to the subject, **you cannot make the process stricter than the law**, but you may obviously make it more lenient. The bottom line is that if it should go so far that the employee is facing dismissal, he or she **mus**t be abundantly clear – **abundantly clear** beyond any reasonable doubt and possible misunderstanding, where in the process they stand.

Sometimes you will be challenged. Sometimes you will encounter blatant insubordination.

**Do not become upset, and do not take it personally.**

**Keep your cool**. There is no advantage in losing your cool – the only thing you achieve is **losing your power**. With your **cool** intact, your **power** is intact. **Do not** let the rest of the team see that your cage can be easily rattled.

Simply go about your normal procedure as described in the agreement from the hiring process. There is **no difference** in that procedure, even if the team member gets personal with you. Just **brush it off and do what you do**, in a professional manner.

Write up a disciplinary report, bring the team member into your office, read it to him or her, ask if they agree or not, note their reaction on the document and have it signed. If the person refuses to sign, simply put: *Refused to sign.*

If it happens again, now you know you are facing a situation where the employee may refuse to sign. The solution is very simple. **Bring a witness**, and let the witness sign, while the employee's contribution will still be: Refused to sign.

**Why do employees put themselves in the situation of having to be disciplined?**

This is what you should try to find out. It could be many different causes under the surface you may never reveal. The employee may have trouble in other sectors of his or her life influencing their moral at work. Sometimes employees want to show off how they can challenge the manager and get away with it.

Try to find out what it is. Is this an employee you have invested a lot in, and who normally performs very well? You do not want to lose this member, if you see a way to rectify the problem for the best of the both of you. If the employee opens up to you, explains what happened and show a genuine will to improve – go with that.

If you encounter this as a new manager in an old company, may be certain employees are entrenched in old ways, and refuse to follow the way you envision. May be they test you, to see how far they can go, and may be they try to put obstacles in your way to make you look bad to upper management. Then you have to take out your least favorable option of management:

× *Be good to the god guys and bad to the bad guys.*

This does **not – and I repeat not -** mean that you use your management position as a platform to exercise power over your team members just to show them that you can. As I mentioned in an earlier chapter – **you do not have to demonstrate your power** – everybody already knows you are in possession of it.

What it means is that for your **good** team members, you may extend **certain privileges and advantages** because they are going the extra mile to adhere to the company guidelines, are maintaining excellent internal relationships and performing superior customer service.

Those privileges and advantages are **not** for team members who consistently challenge you, leave you to clean up their mess or put obstacles in your way.

# HIRING AND FIRING

When you move into a management job, do not make any premature statements about what you will do, and what to expect. You will be given somewhat of a honeymoon. Use the honeymoon to get ahead of the game. Work hard, so when it is over, you are prepared.

Your strategy will be made up of what you find.

**Study the history of the operation. Do a thorough research into the state of affairs in the section of your part of the company, what the situation is and why.**

What has led the section to this stage? Are the factors obvious and **can they be manipulated** – how much, how quickly, and by whom?

**But most importantly:**

When you find the direction –

is your present team willing and able to go where you want to go? If not, you have to make preparations for improvement. Create standards for where your team needs to be, and start the improvements. Interview every one of them to find out -

**What they are doing and how they are doing it?**

**Do they have good suggestions as to how to do it differ-**

rently?

**Are there clear goals for improvement? If not, they have to be created.**

**Does the team <u>care</u> about making improvement? If not, they need to be held to the improvement standard <u>you create,</u> until they succeed or fail.**

Set a track with benchmarks along the way, towards a clear goal you want to reach. Follow up, making it impossible to stray off the road.

Should any member of your team fail to participate in the improvements, and decide to leave, you have to recruit.

**Recruiting is one of the most difficult tasks to do well –**

but **YOU** should do it. It should **not** be left to outside recruiters, sending you a pre-screened field where some of the candidates you might have wanted to see, are already weeded out. **YOU** want to see the applications.

To see **how** they are written, is as important as **what** they say. It will give you an impression of the person writing. Read applications thoroughly, until you get a feeling for the applicant.

Once I received an application where the applicant had been manager at three different stores. In his application he noted that, at the first store he had been a **manager**, at the next store he had been a **manger**, and at the last one a **mager**.

If you are in need of somebody who is not a sloppy writer but in perfect command of the English language, this applicant may cause you problems.

You also need to look for gaps in employment history, and ask **why**.

Interview at least two times, but do it quickly. You will lose interested applicants if they have to go through 3 interviews in the course of a month. Even if they like your company – when they are temporary unemployed they need to make money – anywhere. They will take other jobs – they will **have to** take action to survive.

Always ask open ended questions, making the applicant open up to you –

What did you do in your previous job?
Can you tell me something about your previous managers?
Can you tell me what you liked and disliked about your previous two jobs?

× *Put attitude over aptitude.*

Ask questions where the answers will tell you how the applicant thinks and feels, and **find out what the attitudes are**.

It is great if he or she comes with a perfect education, a ready-made set of skills and knows the details of the job inside and out – but **that counts for nothing** if they enter your customers' homes with a **less than positive attitude**. If their attitude is such that they would rather stay at home, go to the race track or to the bar – **who needs their set of**

**skills**? The most brilliant people can be the most trouble-some employees. It all depends on their attitude.

× *You can teach somebody a job, but you cannot teach attitudes.*

**You** know which attitudes are needed to do the job satis-factorily – so **you** find out which attitudes the applicant has, and if they are compatible with the job. **You** are going to be the applicant's manager –

**find out who you want to manage.**

You start to find that out during the **multiple interview process**. The applicant's attitude to the **interview itself** can often be revealing. Is he or she -

**Late** for the interviews?
**Bored or uninterested** during the second interview?
Answer in much shorter sentences and **does not bother expanding on the answers**, like during the first interview?
Seem **distracted** and eager to get the interview over with?
Express an **overly relaxed body language**, not showing attentiveness?

This applicant is sending **clear signals** that the attitudes are **not what you are looking for**.

Do an interview early on a Saturday morning. The appear-ance of the applicants **in your office** on that Saturday mor-ning is how they are going to look and act **at your custo-mers** on any given Saturday morning.

**Are they bright eyed and bushy tailed, or do they have**

**a hangover?**

**Is this a person you would like to represent <u>you</u> at your customers?**

**Does this person seem to be an extension of <u>you</u>?**

**Will the image he or she portrays be the image <u>you</u> would like to portray at your customers?**

You want your team members to behave **in your spirit** at your customers, showing the attitude **you** would show.

Sometimes applicants will advance through the interview process with an apparent good attitude, for it to radically change once they have landed the job. This is why you have a trial period and you should use the trial period to keenly look at how the applicants are doing.

Do they function well in the team?
Are they on time?
Do they follow proper dress code?
Are they friendly, open and willing to work with you or their assigned trainer?
Are they attentive to what they are being taught?
Are they distracted by an array of things other than work during the day (phone calls, texts etc.)?
Do they constantly talk about a lot of non-work related issues, impeding the training?
Do they give the impression that the most important thing is to get home from work?

There are 50 more questions you can ask about new employees' attitudes – details which **you** as a manager will

**get a sense for and pick up on** during the training period.

It is extremely important that you put together the information you gather about what you see and what you hear and **make a decision** – to either **fully commit** and go ahead with the new employee, **or** during the training period confirm that the relationship **is not going to work out**.

Some of the questions you ask applicants should be **exactly the same** at each interview,

**to see if you get the same answers.**

This is **very** important, because as different answers emerge, you will discover skewed stories, issues which may be hidden or flat out lies.

**Always do medical and criminal background checks, and check the status of the driver's license.**

I have had applicants who at the interviewing table stated that their driver's licenses were suspended. Upon question about how they managed to get to my office, the answer was: "I drove". For a job where it was necessary to have a clean driving record, they showed up to an interview with NO driver's license, expecting to be considered for the position.

This tells you how detailed your interviewing technique has to be, when you inquire about all aspects concerning the applicants.

I had another applicant who volunteered the information that he had been convicted of second degree murder. Are these applicants compatible with the job you want them to do?

**You** decide.

Thirty years ago I could not fire anybody to save my life. I always felt that I was doing something to them which, if done to me, would have been wrong and would have made me feel really bad. The difference I did not see was – **they** were **not** me.

They had chosen to do something that their job description specifically stated was not compatible with how the job was to be performed. Not only that, they had done it several times, after warnings.

In learning management I soon found out that a very common human trait is something I call "wiggling". You secure a job, and then you start to wiggle. You enlarge your personal space by wiggling in a way that you allow yourself – slowly but surely – to do things that technically are not allowed according to your job description. Doing it more and more, without anybody reacting, soon makes it a habit. It becomes a habit **not only** to do that specific thing, but it becomes a habit that **assuming new behavioral patterns is OK**, and will even be defended by the "perpetrator", as the right thing to do.

This is what **you** have to **MANAGE**.

× *You cannot change people - only manage their behavior.*

Can you manage the behavior you see – the wiggling? Is it

a major problem – or is it minor?

The job description has to be crystal clear, taking all eventualities into consideration. If it is not, **have it changed**, to reflect all the eventualities you know to exist.

Stick to it.
Unflinchingly.
Enforce it.
Do not let a single behavioral change which you **clearly** can see will affect your operation negatively, slip through.

You may discover that a member of your team is doing things that seem out of nature – something you have specifically told him or her not to do. It happens again and again, but it is hard to believe, because this employee otherwise seems to do very well. Still the pattern keeps repeating itself, however much you refuse to accept what you se.

× *If it walks like a duck, behaves like a duck and sounds like a duck, IT IS A DUCK.*

Believe what you are looking at, and deal with it.
Instantly.

Address it, **first** verbally. Ask open ended question to make the team member talk about what is happening and why. Ask the questions approaching the issue from many different angles, so you are sure to understand the meaning of the answers, and if they correlate to each other.

Avoid the pitfall of **assuming to know** the answers to your own questions.  Even if you **think** you do -

**the team member has to answer them.**

Sometimes the employee is **very** hesitant about opening up to give you an answer. <u>**Do not**</u> **volunteer the answer yourself**. If the answer you volunteer is wrong, the employee will still go with it, **to get out of the situation**, and the interview will **veer off** in a wrong direction.

Ask the question – then wait. **Do not talk**. Silence is a **very** powerful tool when used as psychological pressure.

× *The one who speaks first, loses!*

Make sure it is **not you**.

If the behavior continues, address it in writing. Get a **commitment** from your team member that it will **not** be a repeated event.

If it still is, you may have to go to the unfortunate step of parting ways. You should **not** be inclined to do that unless you absolutely have to – it is a long, laborious and expensive task to educate and train members of your team. You **do not** want them to fail, and you **must do** your uttermost for that not to happen.

However, if you can clearly see that no other option is left – act.

**Act swiftly and decisively**,

to cut your costs and prevent potential damage among your internal and external customers.

From this follows that the process of separating ways is **not** something **you** do to members of your team. It is something **they** do to **themselves**. The **only** thing you can do is to make all opportunities available for them to adhere to the job description. If they **refuse**, then the responsibility for the separations falls on **their** shoulders, **not yours**. **You** are only the one executing it, as a natural part of **your job.**

May be it can be summarized for the team member in the simple concept of:

**You can do anything you like – but you cannot do it in this job. It has a job description which needs to be adhered to.**

# LEARN IN SMALL OPERATIONS

Where and how do you want to start out on your path to become a successful manager?

**It is easiest to learn in small operations.**

Do not bite over more than you can chew. In small operations patterns are crystal clear, transparent and easy to see. Later you can use what you learned on a larger scale.

The principle is **exactly the same** if you are one, two or several tiers away from the actual external customers. You still have a network around you, which is in contact with the next network – **you always communicate most with your first tier of internal customers**. That is where you get your information, and execute your decision making. The principles are the same – **interpersonal relationships**.

**No difference.**

**Now, go and be the best you can be – apply yourself at management!**

www.ingramcontent.com/pod-product-compliance
Lightning Source LLC
Chambersburg PA
CBHW070820180526

45168CB00002B/696